TO:

_____

FROM:

_____

DATE:

_____

Everyday Sacred

J O U R N A L

Created by Sue Bender

Illustrations by Sue and Richard Bender

Photographs by Kalen Meyer

HarperSanFrancisco

A Division of HarperCollins*Publishers*

I am enormously grateful to all who have blessed me with their bowls.

– Sue Bender

Book design by Gordon Chun Design

Photographs by Kalen Meyer

EVERYDAY SACRED JOURNAL. Copyright © 1998 by Sue Bender. All rights reserved. Printed in the United States of America. No part of this book may be used or reproduced in any manner whatsoever without written permission except in the case of brief quotations embodied in critical articles and reviews. For information address HarperCollins Publishers, 10 East 53rd Street, New York, NY 10022.

HarperCollins Web Site: http://www.harpercollins.com

HarperCollins®, ⏢ ®, and HarperSanFrancisco™ are trademarks of HarperCollins Publishers Inc.

FIRST EDITION

ISBN: 0–06–251543–8

98 99 00 01 02 RRD(H) 10 9 8 7 6 5 4 3 2 1

INSPIRATION FOR TODAY:
Do more than exist; live. Do more than touch; feel. Do more than look; observe. Do more than read; absorb. Do more than hear; listen. Do more than listen; understand. Do more than think; ponder. Do more than talk; say something.

— John H. Rhoades

"We do not great things, we do only small things with great love."
– *Mother Teresa*

INTRODUCTION

If I had known in the beginning what I was looking for, I would not have written *Everyday Sacred*. I had to trust there was a reason I had to write, and I didn't have to have it all figured out in order to begin. I would find what I was looking for along the way.

I hope you will use this journal in *your* search.

Like *Everyday Sacred,* this journal is guided by the image of a bowl.

A begging bowl.

In the Zen Buddhist tradition, a monk starts out each day with an empty bowl in his hands and whatever is placed in the bowl will be his nourishment for the day. Each day is a fresh start.

This bowl is a rich metaphor for life.

Is my bowl full?

Is it overflowing?

Is there room for anything new to come in?

To learn about everyday sacred, we can begin by emptying our bowls. We can begin by noticing the small details of our lives.

What might have been there all along that we've been unable to see? What have we taken for granted?

When I started my journey I was hoping to find a miracle, one that might dramatically change my life. What I found was far more important: the extreme importance of small things.

We don't have to keep searching "out there," or go to exotic places to find what we've been looking for. We don't have to pack a suitcase for this journey. The journey to make each day count is a journey we all can take.

And, each day truly is a fresh start.

How to Use This Journal

There are no rules.

Trust—on the deepest level—that you know what is best for you.

Write and write. Don't judge.

Be ready to make a mess.

Be ready for surprises.

Stop and ask yourself: What really matters? Keep that question alive.

Leave room for the unexpected.

Remember: not risking can also be a risk.

There is no "right way" to be, and there is no "right way" to use this journal. Some people will want to keep the pages blank. Some will use the book as a meditation, daydreaming about the thoughts and spirit coming through the pages. Some are already expert at journaling and have their own style. Others might like a few suggestions. Whatever way will make you feel most supported, do it.

Let these pages be filled with all the richness, complexity, contradictions, imperfections, and paradoxes that are uniquely you.

We all know more than we think we know.

Listen when a voice says, "Pay attention."

Be open for surprises.

You will find what you are looking for along the way.

Each step is the place to learn.

Allow your bowl to be open. Open for possibilities.

"It's not pots we're forming, it's ourselves."
— *M. C. Richards*

"The soul thinks in images."
— *Aristotle*

Look at your day the way an observer might.

Begin to see with fresh eyes.

What do I want in my bowl?

What do I need in my bowl?

Work from your heart.

When we begin looking, teachers are everywhere.

Each day is a fresh start.

"I long to accomplish a great and noble task,
but it is my chief duty to accomplish small tasks as if they were great and noble."

– Helen Keller

Most of us don't have the luxury of large chunks of time to do exactly what we want to do. The challenge is to find even a moment when the world stops—and for that moment, there is nothing else.

Little Sabbaths can replenish our bodies—and our spirit.

Break down an impossible task to manageable size.

"Do more of less."
– *Yvonne Rand, Buddhist teacher*

"I'm seeing wonderful things," a friend told me, "now that I can't walk very fast."

We sometimes feel a hunger inside that we don't understand—and can't satisfy.

"To suffer one's confusion is the first step in healing," a friend once said.

Listening to a harsh critical voice inside makes us doubt ourselves—and leaves us wondering why we aren't more content.

"How we speak to ourselves has a powerful
effect on what happens in our lives," Yvonne reminds me.

Why is it harder to accept our strengths than our weaknesses?

Our natural gifts often elude us because they are so obvious.

The best of what we are is more than enough.

Honor yourself—just as you are.

Why is *not doing* so hard?

Many of us live in a world where nothing we do is ever enough.

What is the path from too much to just enough?

"We do not great things, we do only small things with great love."
— *Mother Teresa*

Doubt if you must, but persist.

Don't try for perfection. Good enough will be plenty.

Sometimes we cross the fine line between wanting a challenge and overreaching.

Expectations become definitions.

Bring the qualities you admire in others inside—yourself.

There will always be things *beyond* our control.

There is a sweetness in surrendering to something you will never be good at, and still finding pleasure in doing it.

We can do many of the things we want if we are willing
to give them space and time and patience.

"Why be unhappy about something you can do something about?
Why be unhappy about something you cannot do something about?" Yvonne asks.

A monk accepts what is placed in his bowl—and is grateful.

Stop at the end of the day, even a particularly difficult day, and make a list, a gratitude list.

Begin a generosity practice and see where it will lead.

Too often we take our small acts of kindness for granted.

Good deeds have echoes.

Our gift is in motion.

"Listening is love," a friend told me.

How we receive a gift can be a gift to the giver.

"What you do may seem insignificant, but it is very important that you do it."

– *Mahatma Gandhi*

The best we can do is different from being THE BEST.

Can we practice accepting?

When circumstances can't be changed, we can change.

Just when we've got our whole life together we get another shove—a reminder of how much we do not know and how much we are not in charge.

Why waste time being unhappy?

Can we be open to receive?

When we stop waiting for something "significant" to happen and instead begin noticing what is happening, small miracles occur.

When we trust we are doing something of value, goals and timetables
have a way of taking care of themselves.

If we learn from a mistake, then it is not wasted time.
The only mistake is to not learn from a mistake.

Small shifts in behavior, attitude, and feelings can make a BIG difference.

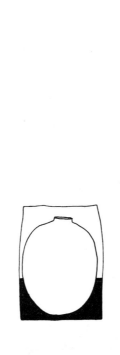

The Latin root for the word "perfect" means only "finished," not "without flaws."

We can learn from everyone and every thing.

Our children, friends, fellow workers—even our most difficult relationships—all are our teachers.

There are no answers, there are just experiences.

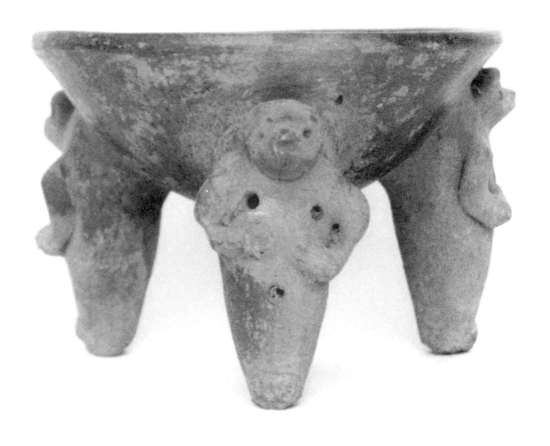

"Allow—for the possibilities."
–utility pole wisdom

Why put a limit on believing?

If you believe, you begin to look.
And you begin to see what has been there all the time.

We all know more than we think we know.

Our challenge is not to do the impossible—but to learn to live with the possible.

Our imperfections are a gift, the very qualities that make us unique.
If we make the shift to see them that way, we can value ourselves—just as we are.

Small miracles are all around us. We can find them everywhere: in our homes, in our daily activities, and, hardest to see, in ourselves.

To be WHOLE doesn't mean we have to be perfect.